Inspirational Stories for Young Achievers

Scientist Edition

Inspire Your Child to Greatness
Through the Amazing Journeys of
Legendary Scientists

Hayden Fox

© Copyright - All rights reserved.

The content contained within this book may not be reproduced, duplicated or transmitted without direct written permission from the author or the publisher.

Under no circumstances will any blame or legal responsibility be held against the publisher, or author, for any damages, reparation, or monetary loss due to the information contained within this book, either directly or indirectly.

Legal Notice:

This book is copyright protected. It is only for personal use. You cannot amend, distribute, sell, use, quote or paraphrase any part, or the content within this book, without the consent of the author or publisher.

Disclaimer Notice:

Please note the information contained within this document is for educational and entertainment purposes only. All effort has been executed to present accurate, up to date, reliable, complete information. No warranties of any kind are declared or implied. Readers acknowledge that the author is not engaged in the rendering of legal, financial, medical or professional advice. The content within this book has been derived from various sources. Please consult a licensed professional before attempting any techniques outlined in this book.

By reading this document, the reader agrees that under no circumstances is the author responsible for any losses, direct or indirect, that are incurred as a result of the use of the information contained within this document, including, but not limited to, errors, omissions, or inaccuracies.

Table of Contents

Introduction 8

Albert Einstein 10

Marie Curie 20

Nikola Tesla 34

Nicolaus Copernicus 49

Ada Lovelace 64

Stephen Hawking 79

Rosalind Franklin 95

Isaac Newton 108

Galileo Galilei 118

Pythagoras 132

Gertrude Elion 144

Leonardo da Vinci 158

Conclusion 168

Claim your free gifts!

(My way of saying thank you for your support)

Simply visit **haydenfoxmedia.com** to receive the following:

- 10 Powerful Dinner Conversations To Create Amazing Kids

- 10 Magical Affirmations To Help Kids Become Unstoppable in Life

(you can also scan this QR code)

This book belongs to

_____

Introduction

Science is a great game. It is inspiring and refreshing. The playing field is the universe itself. —Isidor Isaac Rabi

Hey, young achievers!

Are you ready to unlock the secrets of the universe, unleash your inner genius, and embark on a mind-blowing journey that's cooler than whatever you last saw on TikTok? If so, hold onto those lab goggles, because this book is about to take you on a historical roller coaster ride from zero to science hero in the blink of an eye!

Have you ever wondered about what makes scientists so curious? What drives them to make epic discoveries? How *do* they turn everyday problems into shocking solutions? Together, we'll take a wild ride through the lives of some of the world's most renowned science legends and uncover the mysteries behind their life-changing experiments. These people are the real deal, folks, and if you don't believe in magic right now, you will after you read about these intelligent human beings. Science is like real, tangible magic—the wand is your mind, capable of conjuring up anything and everything.

Not only are we going to discover the greatest minds on Earth, but we will also train to become one of them! In this book, we'll take steps to develop our own science brains, and once you discover your hidden magic, you'll feel even better than you do when you level up in your favorite video game.

So, grab your magnifying glass, put on your thinking hat, and prepare to blast off into a world of curiosity, experimentation, and inspiration like you've never seen before!

Albert Einstein

Imagination is more important than knowledge.

Knowledge is great, but it has its limits. Facts and information help make you a more knowledgeable person, but our imagination takes us further. Imagination has no limits, no boundaries, no rules. Imagination sparks curiosity, and with that comes questions, and with those questions come inquisitive minds that never stop asking, "But why, or how?"

You know that guy you've seen in photos in science books or on posters on the walls at the library—that old dude with crazy white hair? That's Albert Einstein. He was born in Germany in 1879 and changed how we understand time, space, matter, energy, and the universe. He changed the world with his theory of relativity and that famous equation, $E = mc^2$.

You might think that this old physicist who died in the U.S. in 1955 doesn't have much to do with your life now, but his discoveries make so many things possible! Because of Albert's revelations, you can watch TV, play video games, open your garage door with the push of a button, use GPS technology, and so much more! While he did not invent these technologies, he made them possible by sharing his understanding of the universe.

According to many biographies of the famous physicist, surprisingly enough, he wasn't a great student. This is because Albert usually had his head in the stars when he wasn't playing the violin. Instead of focusing at school, he would go on thought journeys or imaginary mind-travel experiments—something he'd continue into adulthood—where he'd imagine himself on a beam of light or doing some other fantastical thing to help him understand the world more deeply.

Always asking "why," he struggled to pay attention in class, but it was this curiosity and imagination that changed the world as we know it today. So, don't be so quick to dismiss the kid who seems to be off in space, because maybe they are! Maybe their unique and wandering mind will discover something the rest of us missed.

Surprising as it may be, it was a gift from his father that sparked Albert's interest in physics.

When he was little, about five or so, Albert's dad gave him a compass. As you probably know, the compass has a needle that is powered by magnetism. Albert played with this compass for hours and hours, watching the needle move this way and that. What intrigued him most was that, when the compass was steadied, the needle always pointed in the same direction—true north. He'd jump around with the compass, trying to see if the needle would point elsewhere when he stopped moving, but it never did. *Why does it do that?* he wondered. *What's so special about that direction?* These questions led him to studying physics when he was older.

With lots of imagination, curiosity, and hard work, Albert discovered that huge objects, like planets, actually bend space around them, which impacts the gravitational pull. Planets, like Earth, have their own magnetic field. Compasses are made of magnetized metal and the two magnets detect each other. This makes the compass needle move as you move. When you hold the compass still, the compass's needle detects the magnetic field of the Earth and points to true north.

This knowledge blew Albert's mind and made him even more curious about time, space, energy, and matter. He would go on to pursue a career as a teacher before truly landing in his spotlight as one of the greatest minds on Earth!

The Theory of Relativity

I'll break down this complex theory that explains gravity with a little fictional story about two space-exploring besties, Max and Albert Einstein.

The two friends had been training for a space adventure, and it was Max who got to explore first. Max was older than Albert and knew the spaceship from the inside out. He was ready to make the big leap, or shall we say, the big burst—blast off into outer space!

Albert remained on the Earth as Max's link from space to life on our planet. He would follow his journey as far as he could and enthusiastically counted down to his friend's very first space trip. Albert watched as Max ascended into oblivion in the blink of an eye. He stared curiously at the sky, marveled by what had just happened—his best friend was up there, floating amongst the stars.

Max had traveled nearly at the speed of light! That's crazy fast.

According to Albert, the speed of light is almost 300 million meters per second! On Earth, the matter that made up the spaceship weighed tons, but in open space, the ship didn't bear much weight at all. So, while time slowed down in space for Max, time for Albert on Earth remained as it always had.

Albert connected space and time, proving not only that the speed of light was always the same no matter how fast you were moving, but also that when things move really, really fast, like Max's spaceship, time actually slows down and space "squishes" in the direction they're traveling. This is where that math equation, E

(energy) = mc^2 (matter) came in handy. For the first time ever, Albert proved and explained the connection between energy (in Max's case, speed) and matter (the stuff everything is made of—you are matter, I am matter, Max's and Albert's spaceship is matter).

So, because of this fact of life, to Max's shock and astonishment, when he returned to Earth, Albert was an old man! He had been traveling so fast that time passed more slowly for him, but down on Earth, time moved faster than in space, and Albert aged—a lot. Now he was the older bestie! And that's relativity, folks!

It's okay if this still doesn't really make sense. Honestly, I don't think we know *why* things are this way, just that they are. It's one of space's many great mysteries, so stay curious, keep asking questions, and never stop imagining. The more you learn about space, time, and science, the more you'll see the pieces to the puzzle that make up our universe. Who knows, maybe you'll be the one to discover the answer to many other great "why" questions of space and time!

Experiment #1: Light Drawing

Have you ever taken a photo of someone playing with a glow stick—a plastic tube that lights up when you bend and snap it? Well, you're about to!

Just as Albert could not see Max traveling through space, your naked eyes cannot see all of the light traveling as you wave a glow stick around, but a camera can! Try it for yourself following the steps below.

Time: At night

Place: In your backyard or in a very dark room

Materials:

- glow sticks
- a camera

Procedure:

1. Have a friend ready to snap a photo, or set your own camera on a timer.

2. Draw a circle in the air with your glow stick. Spin it around and around as fast as you can, and while you do this, your friend or the camera will snap photos.

3. Take a look at the photos and you'll see a beautiful circle full of colorful light! I promise, the photos will reveal much more than your eyes could see. This is because the camera records the effect of stopping the scattered light from the glow sticks.

4. Repeat as often as you like! Add different color glow sticks, connect them together, throw them around, experiment! What other shapes or pictures can you draw with light?

Observations:

Scientists and inventors record their observations to collect data that can propel their experiments forward. Get a separate piece of paper, diary, or journal to record your observations. Also write down the questions below, as well as your answers.

Wonders:

1. What questions do you have after completing this experiment? What do you want to know more about?

2. How could you alter this experiment to yield different results? E.g., What would happen if you used sparklers? A flashlight?

Note: Ask a help from a grown up if you need.

Marie Curie

Nothing in life is to be feared; it is only to be understood. Understand more so that we may fear less.

Have you ever wondered what the inside of your body looks like? Well, thanks to Marie Curie, you can take a look at your bones with an X-ray machine! Marie's groundbreaking discoveries in the area of radioactivity changed the understanding of atoms as we knew it, and with that, interest, experiments, and knowledge in atomic physics grew like never before! Not only did her discoveries lead to the improvement of the X-ray machine, but they also led to the invention of smoke detectors, cancer treatments, and so much more.

Born Maria Sklodowska in Poland in 1867, she grew up in a family where learning was highly valued, and her father was a teacher. She was always learning, picking up books anywhere she could, listening to her father pour over his lesson plans, and soaking up information about the world like a sponge absorbing water.

Some of you reading this might not be huge fans of school, but count yourself lucky because, in Marie's time, the rulers of Poland didn't allow girls to go to school at all. This didn't stop her from learning, though. Marie studied in secret and dreamed of becoming a scientist. She was determined and wouldn't let anything or anyone stand in her way.

I encourage you to think about the following questions and take note of what comes up for you—what thoughts, feelings, or wonders pop into your mind with each question? Note them down in your journal.

1. How might you feel if you weren't allowed to go to school?
2. What would you want to do?
3. What would you learn about in secret?
4. What sparks your imagination?
5. What makes you ask a million questions?
6. When, where, and with whom do you feel the most at peace, the most you?

When you start to find answers to these questions, you can begin to live in a way that supports your interests, values, dreams, and goals, even if you do have to go to school.

Back to Marie Curie! Eventually, Marie's family moved to France, where she was allowed to go to school and learn. This gave her the opportunity to dive headfirst into science. Nothing ever came easily for Marie because she was trying to get into a male-dominated field, but this didn't hold her back. Even though she couldn't gain access to fancy, well-equipped laboratories, she found a little shed that she converted into her own tiny laboratory and proceeded to conduct her experiments there.

Not only did Marie combat prejudice and lack of resources, but she also put herself at grave risk to conduct her experiments. Marie worked with radioactive materials, which would eventually lead to the detriment of her health. Through illness, her curiosity and drive pushed her to continue atomic research alongside her daughter. In 1934, both Marie and her daughter died of leukemia, a cancer brought on by their long exposure to radioactive materials.

Playing With Atoms

You are about to discover the world of Marie Curie and her siblings, born in Poland to a teacher couple. The times they grew up in were not exactly prosperous and happy, as Poland was going through war and internal turmoil. However, despite such an unfavorable environment, their parents made sure the children had an unforgettable childhood laced with games of discovery and fun.

Once upon a time, in a small town nestled between huge mountains, there were four curious and adventurous siblings: Marie, Maria, Sofia, and Joseph. Anywhere these four went, they were known as the scientists. Although they were kids, their adventurous spirit and willpower knew no limits. Always asking questions, trying to figure out why the world was the way it was, experimenting, making mistakes, and getting messy, these four aspiring scientists were always up to something.

Their father was a physics teacher at one of the government schools in Poland. When they were small, Poland was under Russian rule, which stopped the functioning of laboratories in schools! You know what their father did? He brought all the supplies home and set up a laboratory for his children. Thus, the siblings had a laboratory of their own, where they conducted experiments and learned important things.

One sunny afternoon, they were playing outside. Maria and Joseph were building a castle with giant bricks when Marie raced around the corner and exclaimed, "These bricks are just like atoms! They're the smallest building blocks of the universe! They make up everything."

"So atoms are just like the bricks that make up this tower?" Joseph asked.

"Yes! Just like these bricks. But we can't see them," Marie replied.

"Why not?" Sofia asked in earnest.

"Because they are microscopic, that's why. We need a microscope to study atoms."

"But we do have a microscope in our lab!" Joseph exclaimed. "Let's go and inspect ourselves."

"But we can't do that!" Marie protested. "The microscope we have here is a normal microscope. It doesn't have the power to see atoms."

"Let's buy a more powerful microscope then. I have ten zlotys with me," Joseph offered.

"Hahaha, Joseph, we cannot buy one because such a microscope does not exist," Marie laughed, clutching her stomach.

"No? So it is impossible to see the atoms?" Joseph frowned.

"Nothing is impossible Joseph," Marie said, fetching a stick from the ground. She sat down and drew small spheres with concentric circles inside. She was drawing atoms.

"Someone will find a powerful microscope in the future. Maybe it will be one of us, who knows. We love studying atoms, don't we?" Marie said.

"What do these atoms do?" Sofia asked, sitting on the ground.

"They build things," Joseph answered.

"Not just that," Marie added. "Atoms aren't just building blocks, but I think they also radiate energy and change."

"No, atoms don't change, they just stay the same," Sofia said.

"But that's silly if you think about it. If everything is made up of atoms and everything grows and changes, why would we think atoms stayed the same?"

"I guess you don't know until you know," Joseph said. "That's why we ask so many questions. The unknown can be scary or unbelievable until you can prove it to yourself."

"And that's what I'm planning to do. I want to save so many lives by asking questions, making mistakes, and never giving up," Marie said. "I hope I can be a scientist when I grow up."

"But can we girls become scientists?" Sofie asked in alarm.

"Why can't we?" Marie asked. "It doesn't matter if we are boys or girls. To work in a laboratory, you only need determination, willpower, and knowledge."

"But universities don't accept women as students," Joseph contradicted his sister.

"They might not now. But times will change," Sofia replied.

"I'll tell you a secret," Marie said as she huddled closer to her siblings. "I heard father talking about a flying university."

"Flying university?" gasped Joseph. "A university that flies?"

"No, silly! It's a secret university for girls. It operates in secret, without the knowledge of the Russians. We can study there!" she said, turning to her sisters.

"That is amazing!" they shouted together.

"What now?" Joseph asked. His belly grumbled and everyone heard it.

"Well, I'd say we go in for dinner now. Joseph's atoms are growling." Marie said, laughing.

The four siblings went inside for dinner and told their parents all about the conversation they had. Their father promised to show them an experiment after dinner. They couldn't wait to explore the incredible world of science again.

"One adventure at a time, and we will know the whole universe!" Marie exclaimed.

"Maybe we can discover magic!" Joseph said.

"Maybe," they whispered together.

What else is magic, if not being curious and finding answers to the world's mysteries?

Experiment: Homemade Glow Water

A little history before the experiment, just so you know what you're doing.

Marie Curie discovered two new elements: polonium and radium. She named the first after her home country, Poland. This element has since been used as a source of heat in space probes and is highly dangerous for humans to come into contact with. Radium is the element you may be more familiar with as it is the one that glows. Once discovered, radium was used in many ways from treatments for cancer to luminous paint.

So, atoms are made up of microscopic particles called protons, neutrons, and electrons. Ionizing is a process that happens during radiation whereby the electrons are removed from the atoms, changing the molecule. This is what Marie Curie discovered, and it's a simplified way to explain what happens during cancer treatments that use radiation. This process produces a glow.

In this experiment, the water doesn't give off dangerous radiation like radium does, but it will give you an idea of the concept of luminescence and how radiation interacts with matter—in this case, the water.

Let's get into it.

Time: At night if possible (otherwise, turn off all the lights and close the curtains)

Place: Your house or a friend's with a trusted adult around, just in case.

Materials:
- Tonic water (which contains quinine that naturally fluoresces under UV light)
- Highlighters (non-toxic and water-based)
- Blacklight (UV light)
- Small bowl or cup
- Safety goggles (to protect your eyes from UV light)

Procedure:

1. Fill a small bowl or cup with tonic water.

2. If using highlighters, carefully remove the back of the highlighter and pull out the felt ink-soaked core.

3. Soak the highlighter core in the tonic water to allow the fluorescent dye to mix with the water. You can squeeze the core to help release more dye if needed.

4. Once the tonic water has changed color, take the bowl to a dark room or wait until it's dark outside.

5. Put on your safety goggles, turn on the blacklight, and shine it on the tonic water mixture. The solution should glow brightly.

Safety Notes:

- Do not ingest the highlighter ink or the tonic water once it has been mixed with the ink.
- Always wear safety goggles when using a blacklight to protect your eyes from UV radiation.
- Ensure that the highlighters you use are non-toxic and water-based.

Observations: Write these down in your journal.

Wonders: Answer these in your journal.

1. What questions do you have after completing this experiment? What do you want to know more about?
2. How could you alter this experiment to yield different results? E.g., Does the same thing happen to other fruits? What about vegetables?

Note: Make sure to have grown-up supervision for this experiment!

Nikola Tesla

The desire that guides me in all I do is the desire to harness the forces of nature to the service of mankind.

Inventions sound wonderful when they first happen, but after time, they become normal, common, and less exciting. Imagine being a kid when the very first TV was invented. How exciting it would be to go from having no TV to being able to watch all your favorite shows? Nowadays, everyone has a television and they aren't this big, exciting thing anymore. The same with smartphones, right? Though the technology that powers them is quite amazing, we don't marvel over how they work, and we don't wonder just what trials and errors it took to get to the standard of technology they are today; we just use them without another thought. This doesn't mean these inventions aren't marvelous, it just means that we have become so used to them that we don't awe over their existence. But what if we did? How might our minds expand or change if we wondered more?

It is the curious minds, the quirky kids, the mistake-makers, the question-askers, and the imaginative people like you who keep the world interesting, and Nikola Tesla was one of those people too.

Though you might know the name "Tesla" as the title of a sleek car, it was originally named after the genius engineer, physicist, and inventor Nikola Tesla. He was born in 1856 in Croatia. His father was a writer, poet, and priest, while his mother was an inventor (she ran the farm they lived on too). In those days, women often didn't have or weren't allowed formal education, but this didn't stop Nikola's mom. She invented things to make home life easier, such as the mechanical eggbeater! Her ability to think of things that didn't exist, her dedication to finding out how things worked and how she could improve them, and her intelligence and desire to create, inspired Nikola to be an inventor too.

However, tragedy struck the Tesla family in 1863 when Nikola's brother died in a riding accident. Nikola was only seven at the time and began to talk of visions—seeing things that others could not, things that apparently weren't really there. This was just the beginning of his lifelong struggle with mental illness, but this didn't stop him from pursuing his dream of being an engineer. He went on to study at different universities, even though his dad wanted him to be a priest instead. Eventually, after years of studying and working in Europe, Nikola moved to the United States and began working with Thomas Edison.

Anywhere an idea struck him, Nikola would stop everything to sketch whatever popped into his mind. Sometimes that would be on paper or in a notebook, or he'd even use a stick and draw in the dirt on his walks home. His mind was always working, wondering, asking questions, seeking answers, and coming up with ideas that did not yet exist. Back then, he couldn't just record his voice or type his ideas into a phone like you can today, but the reason you and I can do that is because of Nikola's discoveries. Also, Wi-Fi! Nikola's discoveries made Wi-Fi possible.

Nikola was interested in energy through the form of electricity. At that time, no one had invented electricity, but Nikola's and Edison's work helped to expand our understanding of it. Edison is credited for inventing the lightbulb, but it was actually Nikola's work with alternating current (AC) that changed the world, providing homes and the world with useable, safe electricity. With this invention, gone were the days of lighting a home with candles or oil lamps. Edison came up with direct current (DC), which was useful but much more dangerous and impractical for use of things like appliances at home.

Often taking verbal agreements as guarantees for pay, Nikola struggled with money. Edison verbally promised him $50,000 if he could improve his work with electricity, and when Nikola did just that, Edison laughed it off as a joke and never paid him. Nikola left Edison and took his idea elsewhere. You might be shocked to know that before he found another company, Nikola worked for $2 a day digging ditches. From there, he went on to invent the very first water-powered generator at Niagara Falls in New York. This is called hydroelectricity.

He also created motorized boats and something called the "Tesla coil," which was used to send radio waves through the air, allowing the use of radios and TVs. This meant it was the first-time electricity could be moved around without wires. This meant that radio antennas, telephone circuits, and lights were all made possible because of the Tesla coil.

In his lifetime, Nikola held more than 300 patents for his inventions! A patent is kind of like a contract from the government that says that no one else is allowed to invent that same thing or use the idea that inspired it. One that might surprise you was called the *death ray*. During Nikola's time, war had led to depression and the world was on the brink of another war breaking out. Nikola believed he had come up with a way to use particles and electricity to make a dangerous beam. This, combined with machine-controlled boats, he thought, could end warfare as human beings would not need to physically be on the boats. Surprisingly enough, it wasn't believed that this would work and never came to fruition, but the great inventor would still dream of a peaceful, war-free world.

Sadly, Nikola died alone in a New York hotel in 1943. Years later, in 1996, one of his experiments, the one in which he heard messages from outer space, was carried out by a curious group of scientists and proven to be correct!

Jump into the story below to learn more about these mysterious other-worldly messages. It is inspired by Nikola Tesla's work, but is fiction.

Cosmic Discovery

Before the era of television, cell phones, radio, and indoor electricity, there lived a boy obsessed with inventions, science, and all things mystical and unknown. Nico was an interesting kid to say the least. He was always performing experiments in his parents' garage, where he was joined by a few of his friends that were always eager to know what he was up to.

"What exactly are we doing today?" one of his friends questioned, peering into the garage.

"I'm not sure either," another replied.

"I'm studying energy," Nico replied, barely lifting his head. "Everything has energy, you know. Flowing water, blowing wind..."

"Let's mix these liquids and see—" Nico didn't finish before the vessel broke with a big sound.

The door flew open, and his friends ran out. They were soon stopped by Nico's mom, who rushed across the street to check on her son. He emerged from the smoke with his white coat covered in black soot, his hair standing up on all ends, and his glasses with each frame cracked down the middle.

"Whew," Nico said, catching his breath and rubbing his forehead. "I guess that didn't go as planned."

"I would say not," his mother said with a slight chuckle.

Usually, parents would get mad about this sort of thing, but not Nico's mom. She liked inventing too, and she knew that before any miraculous invention, there would be a series of mistakes and challenges—Nico ran into many challenges and made more mistakes than anyone could count. But that also meant he was getting closer to discovering things!

"What do you say we get this cleaned up and you can tell me what went right before it went wrong at dinner?" she asked.

Nico and his friends smiled and nodded as they gathered bits and pieces of blown-up materials.

The next day, Nico's mom requested that he conduct his experiments in the backyard, possibly 10 feet or more from the house. He was on a quest to harness the power of lightning, and that couldn't be done from inside anyway.

"Just imagine how much energy one lightning bolt holds," Nico said as he played with his friends. "If we can figure this out, we could send messages across the street, maybe even across the world without wires getting in the way."

That night, there was going to be a storm. Nico knew it and he was ready. He set up his contraption and waited. By nightfall, the clouds were dark, the air so still it'd send shivers up your spine. The sky rumbled and grumbled before bursting into loud crashes of thunder and bright flashes of lightning.

"This is it!" Nico hollered, holding his invention up to the sky.

Beep. Beep. Beep.

"That's strange," Nico said. "Lightning doesn't beep, it cracks."

He listened some more and continued to hear the same series of beeps. This sent Nico's mind into a spiral of questions. When the storm ended, he spent the next few days trying to find the source of the beeping he heard.

"Aliens! It could be aliens!" Nico exclaimed, jumping up and down.

"Aliens? Are you saying that aliens exist?" one of his friends asked in alarm.

"Well... I'm not sure. But I swear I heard signals from another planet! I know it wasn't from the Sun or Earth. I just know it," Nico replied.

His friends didn't reply, but stared at him in disbelief.

Nico was disappointed that even his friends didn't believe him. He spent the next few weeks telling everyone about what he'd heard. He thought for sure there must be someone out there who would believe him, but no one did.

However, Nico grew up to be a famous scientist due to his relentless spirit and willpower. Because of his awesome inventions, he inspired a group of young scientists who stumbled across his contraption that allegedly picked up otherworldly sounds. They decided to recreate Nico's experiment, and they too heard the beeping messages. Determined to figure out where they came from, these scientists worked day and night for weeks on end before discovering that Nico had been right all along—the sounds came from another planet, but not from aliens like he'd thought.

The sounds were caused by one of Jupiter's moons passing through the powerful magnetic field! This interaction sent out electromagnetic waves that traveled all the way to Earth. Nico had just been so far ahead of the technology of his time that people couldn't yet fathom that such a thing was even possible.

Nico was a strong character who didn't let other people's opinions and lack of understanding hold him back. Though he wasn't given credit for his discovery at the time, he was many years later. Nico spent his life striving to understand the world on a deeper level, teaching us to trust our instincts, go after our dreams, and believe in our ability to discover something incredible!

Experiment #3: Jumping Goop!

While Nikola worked to harness electricity and improve the world around him, you can learn about the power of static electricity right from your home! No laboratory needed, just a few items.

Time: Any time

Place: At home

Materials:

- ¼ cup cornstarch
- ¼ cup vegetable oil
- food coloring
- a balloon
- a spoon
- measuring cups
- a dish

Procedure:

1. Mix the cornstarch and vegetable oil.

2. Add a couple drops of the food coloring of your choice. Notice what happens. Does it mix? Remember, not everything we try in science will work the way we expect it to.

3. Stir until it makes a slimy liquid.

4. Blow up the balloon and rub it on your hair to charge it up! This creates static electricity. When you rub the balloon on your hair, the electrons from your hair molecules rub off onto the balloon. This gives a negative charge and is attracted to the positive charge in the goop, making it jump and stretch.

5. Pick up a spoonful of the slimy goop and hold it close to the balloon (but not touching it). Watch as the static electricity from the balloon pulls the goop closer. If you get close enough, the goop might even jump to the balloon!

Observations: Write these down in your journal.

Wonders: Answer these in your journal.

1. What questions do you have after completing this experiment? What do you want to know more about?

2. How could you alter this experiment to yield different results? E.g., what happens with just cornstarch on the spoon held close to the electrically charged balloon?

Note: Ask a grown-up for help if needed.

Nicolaus Copernicus

To know that we know what we know, and to know that we do not know what we do not know, that is true knowledge.

Like detectives, we search for answers to the unknown, we use the information we have and expand on it, and we ask questions. To be a scientist or inventor is like being a detective of the universe. There are some things we know for certain; for example, if you were putting a puzzle together, you would be confident in telling someone what it will look like when it's finished. You know you are correct in your description because it's right there on the box. As you put the puzzle pieces together, you prove what you know of the image. That's what the first part of the quote means—that you are confident in what you know to be true and real, and confident in what you've learned or figured out.

The second part of the quote is super important and not always easy to admit: There are always going to be things that we don't know. If we walk around thinking we know everything, we might automatically dismiss new information or argue against it. Like the puzzle, while you might know what the result will be, you don't yet know all the steps you need to take to get there. If you told yourself you knew where each puzzle piece went exactly, I bet you'd get frustrated rather quickly when you realized that you don't know where each piece fits yet. When we can admit that there are things we do not yet understand or know, we leave our minds open for learning, broadening our view, and coming up with new ideas.

True knowledge is knowing that the universe is beyond our comprehension. Possibilities are endless, and what we know helps us understand even more. It helps us to ask more questions and dig deeper.

Nicolaus did just that—he questioned everything, even the things that were believed to be true across the world as he knew it.

Born in February 1473 in Poland, Nicolaus Copernicus was raised by his uncle after his father's death. His uncle ensured that he received an excellent education and prepared him for a career in laws of the church. Unfortunately for his uncle, church wasn't of high interest to Nicolaus, and he chose to study other things instead: astronomy, astrology, and for a brief period of time, medicine and law.

While studying at university, Nicolaus lived with his astronomy teacher, and his fascination with the stars and planets continued to grow and evolve. This teacher, who went by the name of Novara, introduced his students to Claudius Ptolemy, who was an ancient astronomer and mathematician. Ptolemy hypothesized that the Earth was the center of the universe and all other planetary objects, including the sun, rotated in larger, different circles around it. This is known as the Ptolemaic system and was believed as fact for many years, until Nicolaus began to question the theory.

Nicolaus continued his studies some years later in the medicinal field. During these years, the 1500s, it was widely believed that the position of the stars, moon, and planets had a direct impact on human body systems and health. Back then, mathematician, astrologer, and astronomer were viewed as the same thing: someone studying the heavens.

In all his studies of space, Nicolaus hypothesized that the Earth wasn't the center of the universe and that the planets and moon orbited the sun. This is known as the heliocentric theory. Because this theory put into question what had been believed for years, heliocentric theory was not accepted or even published for the public to review until 1943, the year of Nicolaus's death. Once this theory was accepted, that the sun was the center and not the Earth, it sparked a wave of curiosity among astronomers, causing them to question old beliefs and explore our cosmos with a new perspective.

So, if you ever learn something and people don't believe you right away, don't worry and don't let self-doubt creep in; for what is true will always find a way to make itself known.

Read on for a fictional story based on the life of Nicolaus Copernicus, who lived in Poland many centuries ago.

Dance of the Stars and Planets

Flash! A beam of light shot across the sky.

Flash! Another.

"Wow," Nicolaus said in amazement. He was lying on a blanket, staring at the stars.

"Make a wish on the next one," his uncle suggested.

Nicolaus and his uncle were sitting in their backyard, doing one of their favorite activities. His uncle was a priest, and was a learned man who had knowledge in many topics.

Nicolaus stared at the night sky, seeing millions upon billions of stars twinkling but staying stuck in place like a sticker to a page. Just as he was about to give up and go in, his uncle shouted, "There's another one!"

Nicolaus stared up at the sky, and instead of closing his eyes, he reached his fingers up to touch the stardust trail left behind. "I wish I was up there," he said.

"Up in the sky? Ah, we can only dream..." his uncle sighed.

Nicolaus turned around and looked at his uncle. "But if we could travel to space, we could have learned a lot."

"Travel to space? You have a wild imagination, Nicolaus. That is not humanly possible," his uncle replied in alarm.

"What was thought humanly unachievable has been achieved in the past. So, who knows?" Nicolaus replied.

"One of these days, you will...." his uncle did not complete the sentence, but merely smiled at his nephew.

Nicolaus was one of the brightest boys of his class, but his uncle used to receive a few complaints about his persistent nature of asking questions. You see, Nicolaus lived so many centuries ago, when asking questions was not believed to be a right attitude.

"Evenings like these are quite beautiful. But I prefer mornings to evenings," Nicolaus continued. "Mornings have sun shining down upon us. Where does the sun go in the evenings?"

His uncle sighed. Here come the questions!

"I suggest you ask your teachers?" he smirked. He knew how Nicolaus was often reprimanded for his questions. "Nicolaus, the great scholar Ptolemy believes that everything rotates around the Earth. The stars and planets are all part of a celestial dance."

(You should remember that during olden times, it was believed that Earth was at the center of the universe. It was later proved wrong by many scientists, Nicolaus being one. During his lifetime, Nicolaus had to go through many difficult situations just because he believed in truth and chose to stand by it.)

Nicolaus had a puzzled look on his face. "It sounds beautiful, but I don't think I know what you mean. How can Ptolemy be so sure? Did he travel to space?"

His uncle let out an audible sigh. "Nicolaus..." he paused. His uncle had been raising him after his father's death. Nicolaus's uncle was a kind and patient man; however, he was a product of his times. He was taught not to question, but to obey the dictates of philosophers and men of learning.

"Nicolaus, one must not ask such questions. We must not question the writings of learned men."

"But uncle, how will we learn without questioning? How did Ptolemy find out that earth was at the center?"

"Earth should be," his uncle replied. "We are the finest of God's creations. We deserve to be at the center of everything."

"That's religion. But science is different," Nicolaus persisted. "Science is about facts that can be verified by us. Think about the number of days in a week or number of hours in a day. These could be influenced by the wider system of planets and stars."

His uncle stared at Nicolaus, stunned by his nephew's words. "But Nicolaus, it is blasphemy. That's what you are saying."

"No, uncle. Do you believe that God created the Earth?"

"Yes, of course I do."

"Do you believe that God has unlimited potential?"

"I... of course."

"Then how can we say that human beings are the best of his creations? For all we know, there might be more of his creations, more secrets of the universe left to explore."

His uncle did not say anything, but remained pensive, lost in his thoughts.

"Do you see that star?" Nicolaus asked. "It must be so far from us, but it's still visible to us as a speck. How big would that be in reality? If we can see a star from Earth, we could also see Earth from other stars. Maybe in the future, if space travel is possible, we will learn more secrets about the universe."

"Nicolaus, you are a gifted child. I believe you can build your own pathways, rather than following anyone else's," his uncle paused before continuing. "But we should also be aware of the times that we live in. Do not be against the accepted beliefs."

"Uncle, I am all for what you teach at the church. Didn't you teach about the ways of God? Didn't you say that the ways of God lie in truth? I am after that. I will explore the truth."

"I must say this, Nicolaus. You have opened my eyes." His uncle hugged him, and they walked back home while Nicolaus asked a series of questions about the universe.

Experiment #4: Mapping the Constellations of the Heavens

The Earth completes one full rotation every 24 hours. While a camera stabilized on a tripod can capture Earth's rotation with very specific settings and carefully chosen locations—something you can do, possibly from your backyard, is map the constellations to help see the movement of the Earth.

Time: At night, when the sky is clear

Place: Anywhere you can see lots of stars; a wide, open sky view is recommended

Materials:

- journal
- a pen or pencil
- a stargazing app or star chart (optional)

Procedure:

1. Pick a constellation or two to follow. Many well-known ones include The Big Dipper and Little Dipper (Ursa Major and Ursa Minor), Orion, and Cassiopeia. If you're not sure which constellations you can see from your location, use a stargazing app or ask an adult to find out.

2. Pick a place where you can lay down to observe the constellations you've chosen.

3. Draw the constellation you see without worrying if it is perfect or exact. The goal of sketching is to map your constellation as the Earth rotates on its axis. For example, if your constellation is at the tip of a tree or building now, draw the tree or building too.

4. Record the date and time of your observation. This will help you see how the constellation appears to move

across the sky (but really, it's the Earth's rotation).

5. Observe the changes over a period of hours or choose to view your constellation at a different time each night.

6. Sketch and label each observation and watch how your drawing changes—this is real evidence of Earth's rotation!

7. Repeat this experiment as many times as you wish. You can follow different constellations, or view them from different locations.

Observations: Draw the constellations you've chosen and record your discoveries.

Wonders: Answer these in your journal.

1. What questions do you have after completing this experiment? What do you want to know more about?

2. How could you alter this experiment to yield different results? E.g., ask a friend or family member in a different part of the world to map constellations and compare your observations. Can you both see the same constellations?

Note: Ask a grown up for help with this experiment if you need it.

Ada Lovelace

*Imagination is the Discovering Faculty, pre-eminently.
It is that which penetrates into the unseen worlds
around us, the worlds of Science.*

The quote above came from a question Ada pondered in 1841: What is imagination? She believed that it was the necessary component linking the unknown with science. Imagination allows the mind to see things that are not there, come up with new ideas, create connections that lead to marvelous inventions, and answer questions that provide insight into existence, purpose, and the way of the world. Without imagination, inventors wouldn't exist and life would be extremely difficult and boring.

So, whenever someone says, "You have an overactive imagination," thank them! Know that this is a huge compliment, a sign of your intelligence and your ability. Hold onto and expand your imagination for as long as possible, for a lifetime! It is those with overactive imaginations that become the great minds that change the world.

Ada Lovelace, originally Ada Byron, never let anyone squash her imagination, not even her mother who believed that Ada's overactive imagination would hinder her studies. In fact, Ada used imagination to develop what many call the first computer program at a time long before computers existed! You might ask yourself, "How could she develop a program for something that didn't even exist in her lifetime?" The answer to this and many other questions is always *imagination*.

Born in 1815 to Lord Byron the poet and Annabelle "Lady" Byron the education pursuer, Ada Lovelace was destined for greatness. Stories of Ada's family vary from her father leaving when she was a baby to her mother taking her away from the family home in efforts to protect her from her father's influence. Either way, Ada grew up with her mother, then her grandmother, and was eventually left on her own at a very young age. However, the women in her life led her down a path of brilliance. With private tutors, Ada studied music, languages, arithmetic, and more during a time when many women were not allowed to study at all.

Ada excelled at math and science, and when she turned 17 in 1833, she met Charles Babbage who was a mathematician and inventor. Typically, Ada would not have had this opportunity to work with Babbage, but because of her high social status in society, she was permitted to do so. They met at a party and Babbage babbled on and on about his newest invention, the "difference engine." This machine was kind of like a giant calculator. Ada was intrigued and quickly began working with Babbage on his machines. Her first task was to translate work from his French engineer into English. She took this as an opportunity to also add her own notes, signing them all with her name.

While Babbage and Ada didn't receive the funding to actually take the difference engine from paper ideas to a real, tangible machine, Ada's notes were rediscovered many years later. Though the original idea was that of Charles Babbage, the notes that made this fancy calculator into a working computer were those of Ada Lovelace. She died in 1852, and her notes did not resurface until over 100 years later!

It wasn't until 1953 that Ada's notes were published in a book about digital computing. Even though computers didn't exist in her time, she is often called the first computer programmer as it was her notes that showed knowledge well beyond her years—that computers work by following patterns. In 1979, Ada was honored for her work by the U.S. Department of Defense, who named their new computer language *Ada*.

Dive into the fictional story below to learn more about how this female pioneer paved the way for the invention of computers.

A New Language

This is a story about a little girl named Ada, and how her curious and clever nature led to one of the most miraculous inventions of our period.

As a young girl, Ada was obsessed with math and science, always pouring over calculations, theories, and experiments in her room that was high at the top of a tower—the only bright blue tower in the village. While other kids would knock on the door numerous times a day asking for Ada to come out and play, the answer was always the same: "I can't! I'm on the brink of discovery!"

Her friends would roll their eyes and ask to see what she was working on, peeking their heads through the door, but Ada was always the same. "You can't come in until I'm finished. When I'm finished, the world as you know it will change. I'm going to blow everyone's minds!"

Just then, a long creak would sound from her room, followed by a *crash!* and *clang!* of metal pieces. To the utmost surprise of her family, Ada would run from her room unscathed, albeit quite sad to see her experiments failed.

However, Ada was an imaginative girl, and was not easily swayed by failed experiments. While most children would have cried over a broken invention that had taken weeks to build, she saw opportunities to make them better. Before picking up the pieces, she looked at them and made images in her mind as to how they could be put back together.

As time passed, Ada saw herself being interested in the making of calculators. She pored over old textbooks detailing the creation of the first calculators. First, there was the Pascaline, invented by Blaise Pascal in the 1600s. However, that machine could only perform mathematical functions of the simple kind. Ada's mind was fixated on discovering a machine that performed calculations of the complex kind. In fact, her genius mind was predicated on a machine that could work according to human emotions! Imagine envisioning such a machine in the 19th century!

However, Ada did not know how to proceed or shift her thinking from a machine that performed simple functions to a machine that did complex calculations.

As she sat wondering, she did not notice a slew of butterflies entering the room through the open window. One fluttered across the book, then another, and another, until she finally looked up to see her room filled with beautiful butterflies. She marveled at their beautiful wings, noticing the patterns, colors, and symmetry.

"Patterns!" she exclaimed. "That's it!"

Ada began drawing patterns of all kinds: shapes, colors, lines, letters, numbers. She drew pattern after pattern and learned that so much of our world, machines, nature, and otherwise operate on patterns. She worked for days in her room at the top of the tower, ignoring knocks on the door, only exiting the room for meals and snacks. Finally, after weeks and weeks of work, she emerged with her hair disheveled, her clothes stained with paint and rust, and her eyes sleepy but full of excitement.

"EUREKA!" she shouted. The sound echoed through the tower and out into the town below, drawing her friends near.

"Ada, we haven't seen you for the longest time," her friends exclaimed. "What happened to you?"

Ada looked at her reflection in a mirror, and smoothed out her hair.

"Come, come," she said, pulling her friends into the room. "Look at what I've made!" she said upon entering the room, revealing a sheaf of papers, all strewn with her writings and drawings of patterns.

"What are these scribblings?" Susan, one of her friends, asked.

"Scribblings? These are my findings!" Ada sounded exasperated. She started explaining the invention to her friends. "You see, everything happens in a pattern. If you look around, you will see patterns everywhere. On butterfly wings and bird feathers alike! Similarly, the answers to many questions lie in patterns. See the patterns here—using these patterns, one can make a machine do things."

"Like?" Susan asked.

"Like... play music, for instance," Ada replied. "Or write messages. Even perform calculations."

"You have got to be kidding me." Her friends were not ready to believe her.

"I'm serious! There is nothing we can't do with mathematics."

The friends stared in amazement and no one spoke. Their mouths dropped open as they listened to Ada explain the new language she had invented.

They did not know it back then, but they were hearing about an invention that would begin to change the world as they knew it.

"I call it, CODE!" Ada said. "Code. Patterns of numbers that tell the machine to produce different results: music, letters, images, movement, you name it. I can talk to a machine and make it happen."

"Will the machine make me dinner?" one friend asked in earnest.

"Will the machine braid my hair?" another one asked.

"I want a machine that would fetch me pastries," quipped a third one.

Ada thought to herself for a moment. "Um, I don't know about machines that can braid hair and make food. But nothing is impossible! If you can imagine it, you can make it real."

For the rest of the evening, Ada and her friends played with the idea of a new machine; a machine that would later come to be known as the computer.

Experiment #5: Binary Code Bracelets!

Just as human beings communicate with different languages—which are essentially sound patterns forming words that we give meaning to—so does a machine like a computer. While you may communicate in English, a computer communicates in patterns of numbers. This is called binary code.

For each letter, number, and symbol that you type into a computer on the keyboard, it is associated with a number code. For example, the letter A is known to the computer as 00001; the symbol "!" is 00100001; the number 5 is 00110101.

Time: Any time!

Place: At home

Materials:

- ASCII binary character table (you can find this by googling "ASCII binary chart")
- 3 different colored beads
- string, thread, or pipe cleaners
- a piece of paper and a pencil

Procedure:

1. Find the letters in your name on the binary character table.

2. Record the patterns for each letter in your name, putting a space between each letter code.

3. Assign a number to the colored beads. E.g., purple beads represent the number 0, green beads represent the number 1, and transparent beads represent a space.

4. Cut the string/thread/pipe cleaner to fit your wrist, or your neck if you have a longer name.

5. Begin coding your name using the beads!

6. E.g., the name Amy looks like this in binary code:
A: 00001 = purple, purple, purple, purple, green
Space = 1 transparent bead
M: 01101 = purple, green, green,

purple, green
Space = 1 transparent bead
Y: 11001 = green, green, purple, purple, green

Observations: Write these down in your journal.

Wonders: Answer these in your journal.

1. What questions do you have after completing this activity? What do you want to know more about?

2. How could you alter this experiment to yield different results? E.g., turn this into a game with your friends. Each of you can make a bracelet or necklace using binary code but keeping your word a secret. See if you can use the binary character chart to decode the bead patterns.

Note: Ask a grown-up for help if you need.

There are apps and toys that can help you learn more about the language of coding. For example, ScratchJr and Scratch are game programming apps for kids to use simple commands to create a moving story. Also, Ozobots are like mini robots for kids that you can combine with color codes to make the bot move in any way you like. Happy programming!

Stephen Hawking

However difficult life may seem, there is always something you can do and succeed at.

A baby boy was born to Frank and Isobel Hawking, a couple who were educated, and hence knew the importance of books. They named the child Stephen, who had two sisters and a brother. They were a loving and normal family who loved to read together. Although they had financial constraints, the parents did not let it affect the education of their children. As a schoolboy, Stephen had a group of friends with whom he played board games like any other child of his age. But they also had conversations on a variety of topics, including the mystical sixth sense. Their playtimes were punctuated with the making of model toy airplanes and boats. Stephen constantly wondered how machines worked, and about the unknown aspects of how the world functioned. One of his mathematics teachers, Dikran Tahta, discovered the sparks of a genius in Stephen, and assisted his gang in building a computer of their own! They built the machine from discarded parts of an old clock, telephone, and other electric pieces. Do you know how old Stephen was then? Just 16!

Stephen went on to earn the name of an illustrious student at Oxford, where he went to university. He was not just into books, but he also excelled at rowing, music, and literature. In fact, his physics professor, Robert Berman, once commented that Stephen was more intelligent than several of his professors!

Stephen soon progressed to be a doctoral student, and during one of those days, he realized that he was experiencing difficulty in doing basic chores like walking, picking things up, and moving about. Remember how he was an excellent rower at the university? He found himself unable to row anymore, and decided to consult a physician. That is when he was diagnosed with a condition called amyotrophic lateral sclerosis (ALS). In simple terms, it is an autoimmune disease that affects our muscles slowly but steadily, until we lose our ability to walk, speak, move, or even eat. Stephen was shattered, and fell into a depression. Such news will prove to unsettle the bravest of the lot, and initially, Stephen was no exception. However, Stephen used positive self-talk and motivated himself to get back up. He regained his spirits, and came back to his studies with renewed fervor.

His work was on black holes, an area in space where the gravitational force is extremely strong. His theory explained that mini black holes were formed as a result of the big bang, the phenomenon that led to the creation of the universe.

He used the help of crutches to move around, and when he lost his ability to write, he was intelligent enough to develop a complementary visual mechanism of his own, in which he was able to imagine complex equations with the aid of geometrical figures. In fact, this genius is often compared to the musical genius Mozart, who was deaf, but made excellent musical compositions by coding musical notations in his head! There is something interesting to learn from these geniuses, who made their unfavorable circumstances into favorable opportunities. Stephen also actively participated in discussions to improve the lives of the disabled individuals, and make public spaces more disabled-friendly. Imagine the lives he must have touched as an activist, scientist, and one of the best inspirations mankind has ever seen!

Stephen Hawking is famous for his bestselling work *A Brief History of Time*, but did you know that he also wrote a book for kids? *George's Secret Key to the Universe* is a children's book written by Stephen and his daughter Lucy.

Fun fact: Stephen Hawking was born on January 8, 1942. There is another famous scientist who died on this date. Can you guess? It is Galileo Galilei, who died on this date, exactly 300 years before. A curious coincidence, don't you think?

Now, let's dive into a fictional story inspired by little Stephen's life.

Little Einstein

It was a sunny morning in September. St. Albans school had reopened after the holidays, and the street that led to the school was soon littered with small groups of students, who trudged their way up to their school. Little Stephen was one among them, who walked alone, when he was greeted with a cry of delight.

"Stephen, wait for us!"

He looked back to see his friends John and George running towards him, their hair flying in the air and cheerful smiles plastered to their faces.

"Stephen, old lad! Where were you all this while? We didn't get to see you during the holidays at all!" John said, catching his breath.

"He must have been catching up with his holiday reading," George offered, with a sly smile.

"Very funny George, but no. We had been away as a family. We went for a short trip," Stephen said.

"Did you now? Oh, I am jealous, where did you go?" George asked inquisitively.

"We traveled across the countryside. Dad and Mom showed us around many places, and we had many interesting conversations about science."

They walked steadily up to the school and reached their classroom.

"Do you wonder," Stephen suddenly asked, "about how the world was born?"

"You mean how it was created?" John asked.

Stephen replied after a pause. "I wonder if it was created at all."

"But what do you mean?" George asked.

"There are many secrets to this universe. I feel I should find answers to these questions, discover the meanings of the universe. I should—" Stephen broke midway, as their teacher walked into the class.

"Good morning everyone," Mr. Holmes promptly greeted his students.

"Did you have a good holiday?"

Without waiting for the answers, he continued. "I hope you have not forgotten about the holiday assignments? Now let me have a look."

Mr. Holmes started prowling among his students, casually marking their assignment sheets with a grunt of approval or disapproval.

"Did you do the work?" George craned his neck to whisper in Stephen's ear.

"Of course. I did it first thing before traveling." He fished his assignment sheets from his bag and placed them promptly on the desk.

Mr. Holmes soon reached their desk and stretched his hands for their sheets. He returned the sheets of John and George without any comments, and glanced at Stephen before taking his sheets. His eyes skimmed over the sheets and rested on Stephen's face with a sullen expression.

"How many times have I told you, Mr. Hawking, that scrawling over a paper does not amount to good handwriting?"

Stephen looked at his professor and stole a glance at his sheets. Everything seemed to be perfectly readable to him. "But sir—" he began, but was soon interrupted by his teacher.

"No more excuses! You should see the handwriting of Christopher and Rudyard here." He snatched their papers and waved it in front of his face.

After scrawling his sheets with liberal quantities of red ink, his teacher returned his sheets, and stormed off to resume his position at the lectern.

Stephen could not listen to the class, but stared at his marked sheet instead, which he was sure deserved better.

"Stephen, it's okay," John said, as he put his hands over Stephen's shoulder once the class was done.

"You can do better if you practice. You are the most intelligent chap I ever know," George offered.

"But...but I didn't get the marks," Stephen said slowly, refusing to lift his eyes from his assignment.

"Ah, that remains a mystery to me. You're literally known as little Einstein," George sighed.

They were still comforting their friend when Mr. Tahta, their Mathematics teacher, walked in.

Mr. Tahta's classes were Stephen's favorite at the school. He had a novel mechanism in teaching, where they debated together as a class on theories and scientific facts. He was not a mere deliverer of knowledge, but a facilitator who encouraged them to think differently and independently.

Mr. Tahta was about to open his textbook when he noticed the group of friends huddled together.

"Is there a problem?" he asked, walking to their desk.

"No sir, it's just that…" George fumbled.

Mr. Tahta was an intelligent man. He saw Stephen's assignment and picked it up.

"I see…" he began. "I understand your emotions Stephen. But don't beat yourself up for it. Why, you're one of my brightest pupils."

Stephen looked at his teacher and said disbelievingly, "But sir, my handwriting…"

"Ah, yes," Mr. Tahta winked at him, and resumed. "Your handwriting is a bit messy and chaotic. It could do with a little improvement. But let me tell you of another person with bad handwriting. His name was Albert. Albert Einstein."

Stephen stared at his teacher in disbelief.

"Have you heard about Picasso? He was a gifted painter and sculptor. A genius in his own right. Also had messy handwriting. Do you know why that sometimes happens?" The teacher smiled at his students. "Sometimes, our thoughts are faster than what our hands can process. For such people, their handwriting tends to get messier when it translates their thoughts into written words."

He patted on Stephen's shoulder. "You can make your handwriting better. You are capable of far greater things, Stephen. Mark my words."

When the teacher walked away, Stephen was smiling with new-found confidence.

Experiment #6: Shiny Black Hole

Stephen Hawking is most famous for his enduring research on black holes. What if I tell you we can understand the concept better by doing an experiment on it? It's fun, easy, and interesting!

Time: Any time.

Place: At home. Make sure you have a parent or adult to help you with the experiment. It adds to the fun!

Materials:

- baking soda (about 5 tbsp)
- water
- vinegar
- black food coloring
- donut-shaped silicon mold
- glitter

- a large tray
- a large bowl
- a small cup
- dish soap
- a syringe
- gloves

Procedure:

1. Take your bowl and add the baking soda to it. There are no exact measurements, but for a black hole, you will need almost five tablespoons.

2. Add your food coloring to the baking powder and mix with a spoon. Make sure you are wearing gloves if using your hands.

3. Slowly add water. Make sure you don't add water suddenly, but slowly instead, until it reaches the consistency of wet sand. Make sure the mixture is black in

color, since we are making a black hole! If it looks gray, add more color.

4. Add some glitter for some extra flare.

5. Now scoop the mixture into the mold. Remember to fill only halfway.

6. Once the molds are filled, place them on the tray and keep it in the freezer. We need to make sure that the molds are frozen, so it is better to freeze overnight.

7. Once our black holes are frozen, scoop them out of the mold, and place them on a tray with deep sides.

8. Sprinkle some glitter in the tray.

9. Add some dish soap around the tray. This is for the bubbly action once the experiment starts, so make sure not to skip the step.

10. Now, put some vinegar in a mug. Fill your syringe with vinegar and squirt

into the black holes. You will see the amazing bubbly reaction!

Observations: Write a small paragraph about what you know about black holes.

Wonders:

1. Google pictures of black holes to see what they look like.

2. Look up what is known as a black hole bomb. (P.S. It is what we just did!)

Rosalind Franklin

In my view, all that is necessary for faith is the belief that by doing our best we shall succeed in our aims: the improvement of mankind.

Have you heard about DNA? DNA makes us who we are. Confused? Think about all the different people you know. Your parents, friends, neighbors, teachers, and people you meet on the streets. Think about all the animals and plants in the world. All of us share a common feature. Yes! All of us have life; we are commonly known as living organisms. Life is made possible with DNA, which in scientific terms, is known as deoxyribonucleic acid.

To build a house, we need a foundation or a blueprint. Similarly, DNA is the blueprint of a living organism. DNA determines all of our characteristics, like the color of our eyes, the shape of our nose, the color of our hair, and so on. It is quite fascinating, isn't it? We must thank the scientists who discovered the wonderful facts about DNA, which brings us to our next scientist: Rosalind Franklin.

Rosalind Franklin was born to Ellis Arthur Franklin and Muriel Frances Waley in 1920, in Britain. Quite like Stephen Hawking, her family played a major role in who she grew up to be. Her father, although a banker, took classes at the working men's college, thereby showing a huge interest in education being a basic right. Her aunt, Helen Franklin, had taken part in movements that advocated for women's voting rights, known as the suffrage movement.

Little Rosalind was an excellent student at school who used to find happiness in solving math equations and learning the ropes of science. She was also good at her languages, and eventually grew up to be particularly good at French. During the time of the Second World War, she was working in Cambridge where she did research on the structure of coal and carbon. This research led to her being awarded a doctorate in 1945. While she was working in King's College, her research concentrated on studying DNA fibers.

Now, do you know what DNA looks like? It almost looks like a twisted ladder connected by bonds. At that time, scientists had not yet discovered what it looked like. However, Rosalind's innovative usage of the X-ray diffraction technique played a huge role in the discovery of the structure of DNA. It is a method that records the process in which the x-rays are diffracted, and it is used to determine the structure of the molecule. The Nobel Prize was awarded to two scientists named James Watson and Francis Crick, but Rosalind's role was not sufficiently appreciated during her lifetime.

Rosalind also discovered the structure of poliovirus, which helped scientists to understand it better and come up with medical solutions. Poliovirus is a harmful virus that causes polio, a disease that could paralyze our body! Nowadays, medical science has advanced so much and we have vaccinations that prevent the disease. Therefore, it's important to be grateful for the efforts of scientists like Rosalind Franklin whose discoveries have made our lives so much better!

Fun fact: In 2023, the scientific community reached an agreement that Rosalind played an equal role in the discovery of DNA structure, which sadly was not appreciated during her lifetime. A musical was organized in honor of her life and achievements, titled *The Double Helix*.

Now, let's dive into a story based on an important incident that actually happened in Little Rosalind's life.

A Good Turn

It was the annual felicitation ceremony day at St Paul's Girls' School. The great hall was decked in festive colors, and awards and shields stood gleaming at the table placed on the center stage. Teachers and students were busy greeting the main guests at the entrance, who were ushered into their seats.

Rosalind was no exception, who was clad in her best dress for the occasion. She stood at the entrance with her friends, her eyes wandering in the distance, searching for her parents. "Will your parents turn up?" Belinda asked her in wonder.

"Of course, they should. They're the parents of the best student in the whole school!" Joanna exclaimed, giving a friendly push to Rosalind.

"They might," Rosalind said. "Also, I'm not sure yet if I will get the prize."

"Who else will? You're simply the smartest," Belinda said.

"Except at music," Joanna teased.

Rosalind joined in the laughter. Her rift with the music teacher was well-known in the school.

As the girls stood there laughing, Rosalind spotted her parents walking into the school gates.

"They're here!" Exclaiming in delight, she ran to the gate to welcome her parents.

"Oh, my dear," her mother said as she hugged her. Her father gave her a friendly pat on the shoulder.

"Why don't you come in, I'll make sure that you get the seats with the best view." Rosalind said as she ushered them inside, leading them to the front row seats.

"Why, Mr. and Mrs. Franklin, such a pleasure to meet you," Mr. Wilson, her chemistry teacher, greeted her parents with a cheery countenance.

"You must be really proud today... Err..." He stole a glance at Rosalind, and smiled at her. "Who knows what might happen? Rosalind could get the prize, after all. Er, I must go and help with the preparations. I will see you after the ceremony."

Mr. Wilson left in a hurry, and Rosalind looked at her parents, her face glowing in anticipation. She had been dreaming of this day for quite some time—of getting the Best Student of the Year prize, and making her parents and teachers proud.

The school principal, Mr. Holmes, began the introductory speech, waking her up from her thoughts.

"Finally, the key moment has arrived," he announced, looking around the audience. "The award for the Best Student of the Year is indeed special this time."

Rosalind waited with bated breath, her fingers clenched together.

"Ms. Rosalind Franklin not only wins the prize, but has also won a prestigious scholarship for university. I take this opportunity to congratulate her, not only for her academic excellence, but also for her achievements in sports and games."

Rosalind glowed at the ensuing applause, her heart filled with pride and happiness.

"Oh darling, we are so proud of you!" Her father hugged her tight.

"Thank you Papa. This feels like a good turn in my life," Rosalind replied, happy tears in her eyes.

"A good turn, no doubt dear. Don't you think you can make a good turn in someone else's life as well?"

"I can, Papa. I will make a difference in many people's lives, through science."

"That you will, dear, I have complete faith in you. However, don't you think we should give the scholarship to a more deserving student?"

"More deserving?" Rosalind exclaimed, in confusion and alarm.

"Yes, dear. We can afford to send you to the university, while there are many students who do not have such circumstances. Shouldn't we make a difference in their lives, now that we can afford to do so?"

Rosalind remained silent for a few minutes while she processed what her father had said. It was indeed a glory for her and the school, she thought, and it seemed too precious to give away. At the same time, she thought about what a difference it will make to someone else's life!

She turned to her father. "Papa, I have made up my mind. Let us give the scholarship to a more deserving student."

Her father smiled at her in pride and admiration.

That was how Rosalind's scholarship was given to a more deserving student, who happened to be a refugee, and hence did not have the means to pay for a university education.

Not only was Rosalind a gifted student and a scientific genius, but she was also a good human being with a judicious mind.

Experiment #7: Learning the DNA

We read about how Rosalind Franklin's usage of the X-ray diffraction technique was instrumental in the discovery of the DNA structure. X-ray diffraction cannot be done at home, as it is a complex procedure that requires machines you do not have at home. Don't worry though! We can still learn to extract DNA, which is an interesting experiment to do together with your parents or any adult who can help you get the ingredients ready.

Time: Any time.

Place: At home.

Materials:

- small paper cups
- a glass of saltwater solution
- dish soap
- wooden skewers
- a glass container with a lid (make sure the container is narrow; a cylindrical-shaped jar works best)
- rubbing alcohol (ask your grown-ups)

Procedure:

1. The first step in our experiment requires alcohol to be very cold. So, we need to freeze it overnight. Do not worry, it will not freeze, as the melting point of alcohol is way lower than water!

2. Use the salt solution to gargle. Do not swallow the solution, but gargle it thoroughly, and spit the solution back into the glass. This step ensures that cell samples from your inner cheeks are collected. The solution now contains your DNA! But now, we need to harvest the DNA from the solution.

3. Add a drop of dish soap into the solution. This separates the DNA from the cell membranes.

4. Now, tilt the glass containing the DNA and add alcohol carefully and slowly. Use the help of an adult, who can assist you in adding alcohol. You must be careful during this step, as the two

layers must be kept separated as far as possible.

5. Put the container down and wait three minutes. You will soon spot white string-like formations in the solution. That is your DNA! For a closer inspection, you can use the skewers to carefully scoop it out.

Observations: Note these down in your journal.

Wonders:

1. Would you like to see the DNA of a plant? You can easily do that by substituting your inner cheek cells for a sample of a fruit or vegetable, mashed well before use.

2. Look up what DNA actually looks like and try to make a sketch of it in your journal.

Isaac Newton

If I have seen further than others, it is by standing upon the shoulders of giants.

All the scientific advancements that we enjoy today, from the vehicles on the road to the television sets and mobile phones to the latest technological advancements in artificial intelligence, we have developed as a species. But was this progress possible in a year? A decade? Definitely not. We enjoy the comforts of the present age thanks to those who have walked before us. Albert Einstein once said that Isaac Newton's ideas are the foundation on which most later advancements in physics were built. Newton himself said that if he had seen further than the most, it was because he was standing on the shoulders of the giants who walked before him.

Arguably the most famous scientists in history, whose laws of motion pave the cornerstone of modern physics, Isaac Newton was born in 1643 in England. Newton did not have a smooth childhood though, as a personal tragedy hit him before he was even born! His father died three months before his birth, an event which was to have a considerable influence on his childhood. Little Isaac grew up with his grandparents and attended school, where he displayed sparks of genius by making models of sundials and windmills.

His university education at Cambridge proved to be a significant phase in his life, where he did the initial research on what later came to be known as the theory of calculus. He was also well-read in other subjects, including philosophy and languages.

Newton also made significant contributions in the field of optics. Optics is a branch of science that studies properties of light. He discovered that light, when entering a prism and leaving it, is different in its properties. This means that the prism does something to the light, which in scientific terms is known as refraction. It's a pretty simple term to understand. We've all seen rainbows, right? Rainbows are formed when sunlight passes through water in the atmosphere. When the sun rays pass through water, they bend at an angle, which produces the effect of a rainbow. Newton thus discovered color to be an important property of light.

However, the most important discovery for which he is known is that of gravity. What is gravity exactly? We know that if we throw a ball up into the air, it will come back in a second. If we jump, we will fall back to the ground. This happens because of the force of gravity. In simple terms, it is the force of attraction between two objects that have mass and volume. In our case, the Earth is what gives us the gravity we experience. In fact, gravity is what makes it possible for us to walk around and do things. Otherwise, we would be floating around like astronauts do in space!

Now, I have a quick question to ask you: What comes to your mind when you see an apple? You might think about the saying, "An apple a day keeps the doctor away." Or, you might think about your iPhone. However, it's important to know about the significance that an apple played in Newton's life.

Do you know the story behind how Isaac discovered gravity?

Hint: It involved an apple! So now, let's find out exactly how this discovery came to be.

The Providential Apple

Isaac Newton was a firm believer in nature. He believed that an observer of nature will find things, and that all answers to our questions can be discovered in nature.

We believe that scientists think about complex things all the time, don't we? But Newton thought differently. He believed that answers to the most difficult questions lay in the simple things.

We know him as one of the most clever scientists that ever lived. But Newton thought differently. He realized that the more that he learned, the less he realized he actually knew! In fact, many well-learned people tend to think like that.

One day in late autumn, Isaac was walking in the garden, taking a break from his work. Even when he was walking around, he was observing the nature around him: the golden leaves, the crispy sunshine, and the apple trees bearing red fruit. How serene and beautiful everything looked.

He chose a shady spot under an apple tree and laid down. He was soon daydreaming about different thought experiments when he was suddenly disturbed.

Thud!

It was a ripe apple that fell from the tree.

Newton took a long look at the apple and looked upwards at the tree.

Why did the apple fall down? he thought. *Well, the apple looks ripe, so the stem must have broken off from the branch*, he reasoned.

Before long, he thought about the way the apple fell directly to the ground.

But why did it fall directly to the ground? Why did it not take an alternative direction? he pondered.

His thought spiraled into new directions, which led to the formation of gravitational theory as we understand it today.

He understood that all objects attract each other, which is dependent on the mass they have and the distance between the objects. He naturally thought about the Earth, which is *way* heavier than all objects around us. Hence, the force with which Earth attracts the objects is what makes them fall down. He called the force gravitation.

Gravitation is one of the many things that make life possible on earth. Think about what would have happened if there was no gravitation? We would float away from each other, and no life would have been possible at all!

What would have you done if you were in Newton's place? Would you have thought about what had made the apple fall? Science was made possible because of curiosity, which means we also need to learn to think about the "why" and "how" of the world around us!

Experiment #8: Fun With Colors

Remember reading how Newton discovered that color was a natural property of light? All of you might have seen a rainbow, which is a natural example of this phenomenon. However, we can easily do an experiment at home to understand the process of refraction better.

Time: Daytime; we need to make sure there is a lot of sunlight!

Place: At home

Materials:

- a prism (a triangular-shaped glass object, which is used to separate light into its constituent colors) – can get this from Amazon

- flashlight (optional)

Procedure:

1. Find a light source: Go to a room with a sunny window. The best time is when the sun is bright, typically mid-morning or late afternoon. If it's not sunny, you can use a bright flashlight.

2. Position the prism: Hold the prism up to the sunlight or shine the flashlight through the prism.

3. Create the spectrum: Turn the prism slowly until you see colors appear on the opposite wall or on a white piece of paper that you've placed to catch the light. This is the light spectrum.

4. Observe: Look at the beautiful colors on the wall or on a piece of paper. You should see red, orange, yellow, green, blue, indigo, and violet (in that order).

Observations: Write down in your journal what you saw and what it took to see the result.

Wonders:

1. Certain animals can see even more colors than we can. This is because of how their eyes are built. Using the Internet, look up what these animals can see. Write the answers in your journal.

Galileo Galilei

I have never met a man so ignorant that I couldn't learn something from him.

As human beings, we have come so far in understanding the world around us. We know now that Earth is one of the many other planets that revolve around the Sun. We know that different planets take different amounts of time to make a single revolution, and Earth takes approximately 365 days, which makes one year.

But science took a while to reach what it is today. Several centuries back, science was very different than what it is today, showing that science is constantly evolving and changing.

What does science mean today? Science means making discoveries, knowing more, and exploring more. It encourages asking questions, and challenging accepted conventions. But there existed a time when challenging accepted conventions could even fetch you a death sentence!

Galileo Galilei was born in Italy in 1564. His father, although a cloth merchant, was also a skilled mathematician and musician. Galileo was sent to learn medicine, but he dropped out after four years. This incident was important to his future because he knew his interests lay elsewhere. He went on to study mathematics instead, and became quite successful at the subject. He was soon appointed as a mathematics professor at the University of Pisa.

During his time, studying science largely meant reading the already established philosophy and writings of famous thinkers. Challenging those ideas or experimenting to test their veracity was considered to be quite blasphemous. However, that is the route Galileo decided to take. Like Isaac Newton, he paid attention to the things around him, which formed his scientific temper. For example, one time he noticed a lamp hanging from the ceiling of a cathedral. He observed how the lamp swung, and he noticed that no matter how far or near it swung, it took almost the same amount of time to swing to and fro. This planted a spark of curiosity in his mind, which led to one of his most famous discoveries. It is known as the law of pendulum.

While he was at the university, he decided to question a belief that was accepted as a scientific fact back then. The Aristotelian theorem that heavier objects fall faster than lighter objects of the same size and shape was questioned by Galileo, who took to demonstrate an experiment. While a crowd was watching him, he took balls of different weights and climbed the Leaning Tower of Pisa. He then proceeded to drop the balls from the height, which fell at the same speed, thus disproving the Aristotelian belief. However, instead of being congratulated, he was forced to leave the university since people found it disrespectful. Thankfully, this isn't so much the case anymore!

He also believed that we had a heliocentric solar system with the Sun at the center. As we have learned, this was initially suggested by Nicolaus Copernicus, who was also disrespected by society. Scholars were very adamant on the fact that Earth was at the center of the solar system. However, there were a few notable scientists such as Kepler and Galileo who believed in the heliocentric model.

Although Galileo made several discoveries in the fields of astronomy and mathematics, including the refracting telescope and his observations on the moon's surface, his greatest achievements lie in democratizing science—a feat no one had achieved in his time. Let me explain what I mean by this. His pivotal work called *Dialogues* was one of the first scientific works that was not published in Latin, but in Italian. During those times, works on science and philosophy were published in Latin, the language of the highly educated. This kept the common people from accessing those disciplines. By publishing his work in Italian, he made a significant step in making his thoughts accessible to the wider public. For that reason, Galileo is often called the father of the modern scientific method.

Now that we know more about who Galileo was and his contributions to science, let's read a story loosely based on Galileo's childhood, to see how he developed his passion.

The Boy Who Gazed at the Stars

The 1500s was a very interesting century in Italy, known as part the Renaissance, which was marked by a renewed interest in the arts, sciences, and philosophy.

For Vincenzo Galilei, Galileo's father, the age truly reflected his persona, as he was a man enamored by the power of music and the wider arts. Although he was a cloth merchant by trade, his true interests were in the fields of music and the scientific arts. During those times, music was conceived as more of a scientific discipline. It was taught as a mathematic subject at the universities, along with geometry, astronomy, and arithmetic.

Young Galileo, the eldest of his siblings, often volunteered to help his father at the shop.

"This is the finest imported silk," claimed Vincenzo to a customer interested in purchasing silk for his daughter's dress. "This will be perfect for your girl's dress."

The customer, a man close to his age, grinned at Vincenzo. "But what is this price you're quoting? How about some kind of discount?"

"Discount for the finest imported silk?" Vincenzo smiled. "Ah, how can I say no to you, Ezio? Let us decide on a five percent discount, shall we?"

"Five? Let's make it ten," Ezio persisted.

Vincenzo gave in as Ezio was a long-time customer. "So be it. Galileo, measure two yards of cloth, and have it packed."

Galileo carefully measured the cloth and proceeded to cut it neatly.

"Does he play the lute, your Galileo?" Christophorus asked.

"Yes, he does! His style is quite charming, considering his young in his age. I took him to the court last week, and the nobles were quite pleased with his skill," Vincenzo replied, gazing at his son fondly.

"Ah, I see... So he will be a court musician in the future, I hope. Or will he plunge into his father's business?"

"No, no," Vincenzo hastily replied. "No to both, actually. I want him to learn medicine. He will be the first physician in the family. I see that in him."

"Physician? That is excellent. Is that a painting behind you?" Ezio craned his neck for a better view. "That is a beautiful painting, where did you buy it?"

"I did not buy it." Vincenzo sat up straight, pride filling his body. "Galileo painted it."

"Goodness! So, we are looking at a polymath, aren't we?" Ezio smiled graciously. "Well, I should make a move. How much do I owe you?"

"Two yards of cloth, let me see. One yard is fifteen florins. So that will be..." Vincenzo was soon lost in calculations.

"It will be twenty-seven florins. Considering the ten percent discount," Galileo promptly said.

"That was quick! I see we have a little genius here." Ezio patted his shoulder.

After his customer left, Vincenzo turned to his son. "Galileo, God has gifted you with quick brains. You should use it to become a physician and treat people's ailments."

"Father..." Galileo began. "Being a physician is quite noble. However, I feel that the universe holds many wonders for me to explore. Many answers to seek..."

"Are you talking about your habit of stargazing?" Vincenzo frowned. "There are already established answers for all that. Aristotle and Plato, philosophers who walked before us, have found answers to all the questions."

"But how do we know that they are true?" Galileo wondered.

"True? We do not need to know if they are true. They are in the writings of the great men. It is not correct to question them," Vincenzo responded.

"Father, the truths of our universe are to be discovered. We need to test them and find out. When I gaze at the stars, I feel the vastness of the heavens gazing back at me, and there are so many questions I have."

Vincenzo stared at his son. He was simultaneously scared and impressed. While the prospect of questioning the sacred rules of the universe alarmed him, he could not help feeling proud of his son's intelligence and farsightedness. However, he chose to not continue the conversation.

"Galileo, will you arrange this stack of clothes?" he asked.

"Yes, father." Galileo busied himself with the clothes, while Vincenzo gazed at his son, feeling that he will someday carve his name in the passages of history. He was not wrong.

Experiment #9: How Does It Swing?

We read about how Galileo's curiosity on observing the swinging lamp contributed to the discovery of the theory of pendulum. You might have seen a pendulum in a clock, but if you haven't yet, look one up on YouTube. A pendulum is basically made by suspending a weight at the end of a string. When it is set into motion, a pendulum makes a swinging motion as it is attracted to the center, due to the gravitational force.

In this experiment, we will see how the length of the pendulum makes a difference in how fast it moves.

Time: Any time.

Place: At home.

Materials:

- a roll of string
- a small weight to tie to the end of the string
- tape
- a timer
- a ruler

Procedure:

1. **Preparation:**

    - Cut a piece of string to a length of 1 meter.
    - Attach the weight to one end of the string.
    - Secure the other end of the string to a fixed point like a doorknob or coat hanger, ensuring it can swing freely without obstruction.

2. **Testing the Pendulum**:

    - Pull the weight to one side at a small angle and let it go.

    - Use the stopwatch to time how long it takes for the pendulum to return to its starting position after one complete swing. This is called the period of the pendulum.

3. **Varying the Length**:

    - Shorten the string to 50 cm and repeat the timing with the stopwatch.

    - Record how the period of the pendulum changes with the length of the string.

Observations: Note down the times you observed in your journal.

Wonders:

1. Repeat the experiment with different lengths of string and different weights. Record the results in your journal.

Pythagoras

Above the cloud with its shadow is the star with its light.

The above quote is by Pythagoras, an ancient Greek scholar and mathematician, whose teachings laid crucial frameworks to the modern fields of mathematics. When we think about it, the quote is very inspiring and positive in its meaning. In life, we might come across hardships and difficult times. However, such times will not last forever. Good times will definitely follow if we are willing to work for our dreams.

Pythagoras was born in 570 B.C.E. on a Greek island called Samos. Since he lived so many centuries ago, there are not many valid historical records about his early life. It is said that in his youth, Pythagoras traveled widely, which influenced his worldview and perceptions. He eventually settled in a place called Cortona, in modern Italy. His wisdom and learning attracted a group of scholars to him, which slowly developed to be a brotherhood, known as the Pythagorean brotherhood. During those times, philosophy and religion were not separated from science, and the brotherhood had very strict views regarding religion and morality. They were said to have had cultivated nonviolent aspects in their community, including vegetarianism. It is also said that many reputed scholars of the day traveled to Cortona to listen to the teachings of Pythagoras.

You may have heard of the Pythagorean theorem, which was used by Pythagoras and his followers. Although experts say that the theorem was actively used in other parts of the world, Pythagoras is believed to have introduced it to the world. The theorem says that in a right-angled triangle, the square of the longer side, which is known as the hypotenuse, is equal to the sum of the squares of the other two sides. Don't worry if this and some of the other concepts in this book are confusing and don't make sense yet. Your teachers at school will explain it in detail once you're old enough.

Pythagoras also had an active interest in astronomy. During his time, the shape of the Earth was not known to be spherical; it was instead believed to be flat. He was one of the first scholars who predicted the shape of Earth to be spherical in shape.

As we already know, he traveled a lot and had a wealth of experience gained through traveling and scientific observation. He divided Earth into five climatic zones, which are still used to this day. Like Galileo, he was observant of the stars and celestial objects too. In his times, people referred to the stars seen in the early morning as "morning stars" and stars seen at night as "evening stars". Pythagoras was the first to identify that the morning stars and evening stars were actually the same celestial objects.

Furthermore, his teachings on numbers and mathematics influenced Greek sculptors to build sculptures and buildings according to mathematical ratios, which led to beautiful symmetrical structures. It's safe to say that Pythagoras was an important scientist of his time who contributed heavily to our scientific knowledge.

Now that we know more about Pythagoras, let's dive into a story based on Pythagoras's perceived childhood. It's an imaginary take on how Pythagoras might have been as a curious little boy on a Greek island.

Sailing Ships

Samos was a peaceful island in Greece. The people who lived there were kind and helpful, as it was a small island where everyone knew each other.

Pythagoras was a small boy in Samos, who was well known for his ways of inquiring about everyone's business, asking questions, and wondering about the ways of things.

"Little Pythagoras never stops asking questions!" Herodotus, his neighbor exclaimed aloud. "He wants to know why the sky is blue, and why the cat meows. As if we have answers to everything."

"Tell me about it," his wife laughed aloud. "Yesterday he was up in the trees, hunting for birds' nests. He said he wanted to see eggs hatching. It took us a lot of trouble to make him climb down before he got pecked by the birds."

That's just how he was. However, little Pythagoras was also very helpful to others. He helped old people carry the goods from the market and ran errands for his neighbors and family. He was well loved for his nature, although most of the townsfolk couldn't answer even half of his questions.

One day, Pythagoras was sitting by the seaside, gazing at the blue sea and the ships that sailed on it. This was one of his favorite hobbies because of its beauty and serenity. He was soon joined by his friends Philolaus and Timaeus. They used to pick up shells from the seashore and play various games with them. That day, however, Pythagoras seemed to be lost in thought and didn't reciprocate his friends' invitations to play together. Instead, he asked, "What do you think the Earth is shaped like?"

His friends were a bit taken aback. "Shape of the Earth? Why are you asking this now? Where did that even come from?" Philolaus asked.

"Answer my question. What do you think it's shaped like?" Pythagoras replied.

"Must be flat. Haven't you seen the maps our parents use when they sail across the sea? That is how Earth must look like," Timaeus promptly replied.

"Then it must be a square, or a rectangle," Philolaus offered.

"I think our planet is round, like a ball," Pythagoras said curiously.

"A ball? That is ridiculous. What on Earth makes you think that?" Philolaus asked in confusion.

"Do you see those ships in the distance?" Pythagoras pointed to the horizon. "Those ships move away from us steadily, and when they are the horizon, they are visible as a small speck, which eventually disappears. They disappear because Earth is shaped like a ball. If Earth was flat, they would not have disappeared, right?"

His friends did not reply, but remained gazing at the horizon, transfixed.

"But... but that is not what our elders say," Timaeus said at last.

"How do we know if they are right? Nature tells us differently," Pythagoras said.

As they were discussing, a couple of men walked to the shore. Among them was Artemis, Timaeus's father, who was a merchant.

"Father!" Timaeus called out.

"Timaeus, my son," his father called out fondly, walking to the friends and extending his arms. "Pythagoras and Philolaus! I have not seen you for a long time! Are you keeping well?"

After exchanging pleasantries, Artemis continued. "We are planning to travel to Egypt to source some clothes for the next season. It will take us two weeks for the journey."

"Two weeks! That is a long time. Egypt lies next to the sea after all," Pythagoras exclaimed.

Artemis laughed. "Yes, it seems like it is next to us, but it takes a while to travel by the sea. We need to travel southwards, then shift to the east."

Pythagoras thought hard, and then replied. "But why do you need to change directions, if there is a straight line between the two points?"

Artemis was perplexed. "Straight line? Do you think the sailors and our ancestors did not study sailing well? Pythagoras, you sure do ask a lot of questions. Anyways, it is getting late and I must leave. The weather conditions right now are ideal for the journey."

Artemis and his companion left for the boat, while Pythagoras stood lost in his thoughts.

He turned to his friends. "If we know the starting point and the ending point, we might be able to calculate the shortest distance between them. Here, the ship travels south and then turns east." He took a sharp-edged stone and drew two lines on the sand. "See? This looks like the two sides of a triangle. I am sure we can calculate the third side from this."

"But how?" Philolaus asked.

"That... I'll have to find out," Pythagoras replied, smiling at his friends.

We know what happened after that—he eventually did discover the answer and came up with the famous Pythagorean theorem!

Experiment #10: Pythagoras' Musical Discovery

Objective: To demonstrate Pythagoras' discovery of the relationship between the length of a string and the pitch it produces when plucked, a foundational concept in the study of musical harmony and acoustics.

Time: Any time.

Place: At home.

Materials:

- A ruler or a stick
- String or yarn
- Tape
- Scissors
- A friend or grown-up to help

Procedure:

1. **String Preparation:**

    - Cut a piece of string or yarn about 60 cm long. This will be the length of 2 rulers.

    - Hold one end of the string while your friend holds the other.

2. **Experimenting with Lengths**:

    - Pluck the string near the middle with your other hand and listen to the sound it makes.

    - Now do the same thing again, but pluck it half-way between the middle-point and your hand. Observe the difference in sound!

Observations: Record your observations in your journal.

Wonders: Repeat the experiment with the wonders below and record your observations in your journal.

1. What would happen if you used different thicknesses or types of string?
2. How does the tension of the string affect the pitch?
3. What happens if you use different materials like metal wire or rubber bands?

Gertrude Elion

Don't let others discourage you or tell you that you can't do it. In my day I was told women didn't go into chemistry. I saw no reason why we couldn't.

Have you been told that you can't achieve certain things? Sometimes, we might get told that we are too small or weak or not smart enough. But, do you believe it when someone tells you that? Because what others might tell you is their perception of your potential, which might not be true, unless you believe it.

Once there was a girl named Gertrude Elion who loved her grandfather very much. Like most granddaughters, she grew up listening to his wonderful tales and looked forward to visits to see him. When she was 15 years old though, her grandfather was tragically diagnosed with stomach cancer. It was the early 1900s when treatment for cancer was not as developed as it is today. Although Gertrude remained with her grandfather during his last days, she was considerably affected by his suffering, which left a lasting impression on her. That was the moment when she decided to dedicate her life to researching lifesaving medicine.

Although her family could not afford to send her to university, she won a prestigious scholarship and graduated in chemistry from

Hunter College. After her graduation, she tried for a job in research, but was told that a woman had no place in a chemistry lab. To pay her bills, she worked as a secretary and teacher before her interest in the subject made her go back to trying for a job in research. After several rejections, she was feeling down, but refused to give up.

She stayed resilient and kept trying, and eventually was offered an unpaid position that she gladly took up, showcasing her passion for her field. At the same time, she went back to university to get her master's degree in chemistry, all the while supporting herself with side jobs.

After graduation, she tried her hand at research again, but still with no success. She had to work as a food quality tester before she became an assistant at a pharmaceutical company. Her boss at the company, George Hitchings, was conducting experiments to find a new drug for cancer, which killed cancerous cells without damaging normal cells. Gertrude stepped up to the plate, offering her insights and years of education, and soon proved her intelligence and capability by successfully developing two anti-cancer drugs, thus turning her childhood dream into reality. In 1988, she was awarded the prestigious Nobel Prize for medicine along with George Hitchings and James Black. From a girl who was ridiculed for her dreams and denied a place in the chemistry lab, she went on to become the recipient of the famous Nobel Prize!

Her life stands testimony to the fact that sheer determination and hard work will fetch success, even if no one believes in you. You only need to believe in yourself and you're your butt off, and success will be yours. From the Gertrude who worked part-time to fund her masters degree, she went on to become a honorary recipient of a doctoral degree from the Tandon School of Engineering at New York University. From being refused a space in the chemistry lab, she went on to work for premier institutes like the National Cancer Institute and World Health Organization. She also worked as a professor at Duke University.

Her contribution toward finding a lifesaving anti-cancer drug isn't her only achievement. She also contributed toward discovering a drug commonly known as AZT, which is used against HIV and AIDS.

Now that we know more about the amazing Gertrude Elion, let's dive into an imaginative recount of a day in little Gertrude's life.

The Girl Who Dared to Dream

It was 7 AM on Sunday morning, and young Gertrude was already up and about. It was the day of the zoo visit and she was too excited to sit still. After brushing her teeth and washing her face, she started her morning off like she always did, by reading the daily newspaper. It was a habit that her father had instilled in her from a young age.

She loved to read about what happened in other parts of the world, wanting to go there herself one day. Little Herbert, her little brother who loved listening to his big sister's recount of world news, kept her company, along with her parents. Her readings were often supplemented with commentary, which her family always found entertaining.

"Look at this news. An 11-year-old boy is inflicted with leukemia and is battling for his life. His family is seeking help," Gertrude said, her eyes widened. "That's terrible. He is almost my age!"

This was a unique feature of Gertrude's character. She was genuinely filled with empathy and felt deeply for each and everyone's suffering.

"Is leukemia really bad?" she asked her parents. Her father was a dentist and had good knowledge in matters related to health.

"It usually is," he replied, between sips of his morning coffee. "It is particularly unfortunate when it affects little children. Leukemia is an affliction which affects the red blood cells. You know, the small red cells in our blood?" He paused for a hint of acknowledgement from his daughter.

"Yes, I know the red blood cells. They carry oxygen in our body," she promptly replied.

Gertrude was more intelligent than most children of her age. She regularly topped her class, so this was not a surprise.

"Excellent. So, when the red blood cells get affected, you can imagine how severe it could get, since they perform such an important function," her father explained.

"But... There could be a medicine to make them alright. Just like I have to take medicine for my fevers?"

Her father paused before replying. "Sadly, cancer is not like a fever. It affects our cells, and it is difficult to administer a medicine to destroy the affected cells without damaging the healthy cells in the process."

Gertrude was soon lost in thought.

Her mother gazed fondly at her pensive daughter and gently pushed her to get ready for the day out. "We don't want to be late.

Remember, we're also meeting Uncle Marty at the zoo."

Uncle Marty was their family friend, who had two sons about the same age as her.

Although they set out to the zoo, Gertrude was still lost in her thoughts, wondering about the possibilities of a medicine that could selectively destroy the cancer cells.

However, soon her spirits lifted, as the zoo was one of her favorite places in the city. She loved to see the animals, pausing before each enclosure to read the descriptions. She imagined the zebras and elephants in the wilderness of Africa, and conjured visions of toucans and jaguars in South America.

After walking for a couple of hours, they got hungry and sat down to have a meal at the zoo restaurant.

"So Jim, which animal did you like best?" Uncle Marty asked one of his sons.

"I liked the animal with the long nose. It looked funny," he replied.

"You mean the elephant?" Uncle Marty asked.

"No, the smaller animal," he replied.

"He must be talking about the tapir. They're commonly found in South America and are also herbivores, like elephants," Gertrude offered.

Uncle Marty tended to get annoyed that Gertrude was brighter than his sons, and wasted no opportunity to show that.

"Hah! Seems little Gertrude is into animals now," he exclaimed.

"I have always loved animals," she replied in a matter-of-fact tone.

"Ah, well. Now you can be a zoo assistant once you grow up. Taking care of animals, feeding them, and bathing them," he snickered.

"That would be lovely!" Gertrude replied, failing to see the hidden sarcasm. However, she continued. "But I would like to be a scientist first and foremost. I will study chemistry and invent medicines to help people get better. That's what I would like to do."

This revelation was followed by a silence. Her parents beamed at her with pride, while Uncle Marty made a face then continued.

"That's a noble ambition for sure. Too bad you are a girl, though. A chemistry lab is hardly a woman's place."

"But why do you say that? A woman can do whatever a man can do. I am the best student in my class," Gertrude asked.

"But the world is not your class," Uncle Marty persisted. "Women will not be allowed in spaces like laboratories. How many women you know have made life-changing inventions?"

"I do not agree, Uncle Marty. Dreams should not be limited. If I can dream, I can also achieve. I am sure my name will be one of those names in the future, when someone asks about women who have made life-changing inventions," Gertrude said, confidence brimming in her voice.

"We will see," Uncle Marty concluded.

And see he did! Just like Uncle Marty here, we might have plenty of naysayers around us, waiting to dissuade us from having ambitious dreams. However, nothing can get in our ways or bring us down, as long as we believe in ourselves.

Experiment #11: Acidic or Basic?

We know that Gertrude was a pioneer in the field of chemistry. You might also be learning chemistry at school. If you are, you might already know about acids and bases. Some substances are acidic and some are basic, while others are neutral. Let's do an experiment to determine if certain substances are acidic, basic, or neutral.

Be sure to have a grown up help with this one!

Time: Any time.

Place: At home.

Materials:

- Red cabbage
- Hot water
- Clear glasses or cups
- Various household liquids (e.g., lemon juice, milk, soapy water, baking soda solution, vinegar, or anything else you want to test)
- A strainer
- A knife (to be used by an adult!)

Procedure:

1. Preparation:
- With adult supervision, finely chop the red cabbage.

- Place the chopped cabbage in a large bowl and cover it with hot water. Let it sit until the water turns deep purple, indicating the pigment has been released.

- Strain out the cabbage pieces, leaving you with a purple cabbage juice, which will serve as your pH indicator.

2. **Testing pH:**
   - Pour the cabbage juice into several clear glasses, about halfway full.

   - Add a different household liquid to each glass of cabbage juice and stir. For example, add lemon juice to the first glass, soapy water to the second, and continue with each liquid you've chosen.

3. **Observing the Reaction:**
   - Observe the color changes in the cabbage juice, which will vary according to the pH level of the liquid added. Acidic solutions will turn the juice pinkish-red, neutral solutions will keep it purple, and basic solutions will turn it greenish-blue.

Observations: Write down your observations in your journal.

Wonders:

1. What happens if you mix the altered pH solutions together?

2. How does the concentration of the acidic or basic substance affect the color change?

Leonardo da Vinci

The noblest pleasure is the joy of understanding.

Most of us know Leonardo da Vinci as a great artist who painted masterpieces like the Mona Lisa. But did you know he was also an engineer, architect, scientist, and sculptor? In fact, his contributions to science and architecture tower above anything else, which were discovered from a set of notebooks where he recorded his findings.

He was born in the 16th century Renaissance period in Italy. As a boy, he was taught painting and sculpting by an artist named Verrocchio. This is where he picked up skills in painting and drawing, which formed some of the foundations of his future endeavors. Even from a young age, he had an immense interest in the nature around him, which stretched from the architecture of the buildings to the anatomy of human beings and animals. He kept several notebooks with him, constantly writing whatever interesting thoughts came to mind.

What's interesting to note is that although the airplane was invented in the 20th century, Leonardo's notebooks had intricate drawings of helicopters and gliders, showing just how far ahead of his time he really was. His designs were not only futuristic, but also carried the unmistakable imprint of a genius. One of the unique characteristics of Leonardo was that he had a wonderful blend of both an artistic and scientific mind. He used this gift to make well-detailed and complex designs without sacrificing the aspects of utility and practicality.

An elaborate design made by Leonardo had been lost to the world before it was discovered in 1952. The design was for a bridge, which was to be constructed over Golden Horn in today's Istanbul. Although the design was not made into a bridge, the sheer excellence of the design remains a marvel even today. If the bridge was constructed, it would have been the longest in the world! To test if the design would have been successful, scientists at MIT conducted a 3D model of the bridge. The model surpassed the tests, thus proving the incredible engineering knowledge of Leonardo da Vinci.

Through modern technology, we have made astounding progress in the field of medical advancement. However, during Leonardo's times, humans did not have the means to gain a thorough understanding of human anatomy. This gap in their knowledge was bridged to a great extent through Leonardo's well-detailed drawings. He relied on human corpses, which were carefully dissected himself, and the anatomical details were copied down with the utmost precision. The human skeletal system, muscular system, and circulatory system were revealed in great detail for the first time, which acted as an essential guidebook for future physicians.

Many of you might be familiar with solar power and hydroelectric power. These are eco-friendly and renewable sources of energy, which are harnessed through sunlight and moving water, respectively. Did you know that Leonardo had anticipated these in the 16th century? A few of his drawings showcase solar power and hydropower getting trapped and being used for tasks such as metal welding, which again showcases the depth of his futuristic thinking.

Now that we know a bit more about the mind-blowing achievements of Leonardo da Vinci, let's explore more about his childhood with a story.

The Rose Bush

This story takes us to the 16th century when Italy was going through massive changes brought upon by the Renaissance, a period of history that brought great advances in the arts and science. Because Leonardo grew up in the middle of this time period, his childhood was heavily influenced by the changes of the time.

Leonardo had a magical hand and mind. His paintings and drawings brimmed with life and vitality. His father, quite impressed by his son's talent, took him to Andrea del Verrocchio, who was a famous Italian painter and sculptor.

Now, Verrocchio was not any ordinary painter; he was so talented that his paintings were often commissioned by the royalty of Italy. When Leonardo's father, Ser Piero, asked Verrocchio to teach his son, Verrocchio did not quite like the idea at first.

"I do not teach kids, Piero. I hope you know that." Verrocchio dismissed the request.

"I'm aware Verrocchio, but Leonardo here is not like the other children; he is quite talented at art. If he is given the right guidance, I know he will grow up to be legendary," Ser Piero persisted.

"Is he now?" Verrocchio asked, his tone sarcastic. "Let us test it then. I will give you twenty-four hours, Leonardo. You can choose any subject of your liking and reproduce it on the canvas. Let me see if you have what it takes."

Leonardo accepted the challenge and left Verrocchio's workspace.

Within 14 hours, he was back again, to the immense surprise of Verrocchio.

"Are you done already?" Verrocchio asked.

"Yes sir," Leonardo replied. "The painting is outside. Will you come and have a look at it?"

Verrocchio walked outside his studio and looked around his garden. "Where is it?" he asked.

Leonardo smiled and pointed to a spot next to where Verrocchio was standing.

Although Verrocchio looked sideways, he could not spot anything. However, when he looked again, he was taken aback. What he thought to be a rose bush in his garden was the painting Leonardo had done! It was in the image of a lion and was so beautiful that even the bees were swarming to it!

Verrocchio could not believe his eyes. This was not only beautiful execution by the young Leonardo, but also out-of-the-box thinking. Being a gifted artist himself, he understood the genius Leonardo had within him and accepted him as his student.

Experiment #12: Is Seeing Believing?

All of you must have seen pictures of the Mona Lisa, one of the most popular paintings in the world. Do you know an interesting feature of the Mona Lisa? The expression of Mona Lisa is very difficult to decode. If you look at Mona Lisa from one angle, she will appear to be smiling. However, if you look her from another angle, she will appear to be somber. This is made possible by a technique known as optical illusion.

To demonstrate this, let's create an optical illusion of our own!

Time: Any time.

Place: At home.

Materials:

- A pencil (a regular wooden pencil works best)
- A glass or clear plastic cup
- Water

Procedure:

1. **Fill the Cup:** Fill the glass or plastic cup about three-quarters full with water.

2. **The Pencil Trick:** Hold the pencil straight up and down (vertically) and slowly lower it into the water at an angle. Keep your eyes on the part of the pencil that is submerged in water.

3. **Observe the Illusion:** Slowly move the pencil up and down while it's partially submerged. Watch how the pencil appears to bend at the point where it enters the water.

4. **Experiment Further:** Try changing the angle at which you insert the pencil into the water. Observe how the illusion changes.

Observations: Write down your observations in your journal.

Wonders:

1. Why does the pencil appear to bend when it's in the water?

2. What happens if you use different liquids (like oil or a sugar solution) instead of water?

3. Try the experiment with objects of different shapes and materials (like a straw or a spoon). Do they all show the same bending effect?

Conclusion

Somewhere, something incredible is waiting to be known. – Carl Sagan

We are finally here, folks! What a journey it has been! We met some of history's most incredible scientists and got to know them through their inspirational life stories. There were amazingly talented female scientists like Marie Curie, Ada Lovelace, Rosalind Franklin, and Gertrude Elion—women who were told science was not for them. However, they paid no heed to the naysayers, and instead focused on their goals to emerge as winners. So the next time someone asks you if girls can be scientists, you know what to say, right?

We also met legendary geniuses like Galileo Galilei, Nicolaus Copernicus, Pythagoras, and Leonardo da Vinci, born during times when science was seen in a much different light than now. Never forget that we enjoy all of our modern comforts because people like them dared to think differently during a time when it was much more dangerous to do so.

Albert Einstein and Isaac Newton are synonymous with modern science for their pivotal contributions that will never lose relevance. And how can we forget Nikola Tesla and Stephen Hawking, who had giant hurdles to climb, but emerged victorious nevertheless.

Although their times and circumstances are different from each other, there is a common factor that connects all of these scientists together. Can you guess?

It's their sheer willpower, relentless work ethic, and boundless curiosity. They observed their surroundings carefully, dared to ask questions, and had a deep desire to explore the unknown. Did you notice the quote above? It is by Carl Sagan, a famous astronomer whose words should serve as an inspiration to all of us. Somewhere, something is waiting to be known and there's a good chance you could be the one to discover it. Thank you for reading young achievers. May you go on to achieve greatness!

Leave Your Feedback on Amazon

Please think about leaving some feedback via a review on Amazon. It may only take a moment, but it really does mean the world for small authors like myself :)

Even if you did not enjoy this title, please let me know the reason(s) in your review so that I may improve this title and serve you better.

From the Author

As a retired school teacher, my mission with this series is to create premium educational content for children that will help them be strong in the body, mind, and spirit via important life lessons and skills.

Without you, however, this would not be possible, so I sincerely thank you for your purchase and for supporting my life's mission.

Don't forget your free gifts!

(My way of saying thank you for your support)

Simply visit **haydenfoxmedia.com** to receive the following:

- 10 Powerful Dinner Conversations To Create Amazing Kids

- 10 Magical Affirmations To Help Kids Become Unstoppable in Life

(you can also scan this QR code)

More titles you're sure to love!

Printed in Great Britain
by Amazon